W9-BHZ-867
3 1230 00685 0297

Dazzling Dragonflies

A Life Cycle Story

Linda Glaser

Illustrations by
Mia Posada

Millbrook Press • Minneapolis

To Kurt Mead, author of *Dragonflies of the North Woods*. Many thanks for sharing your dazzling expertise!

—LG

To Raul with love—and to our family, now and to be

—MP

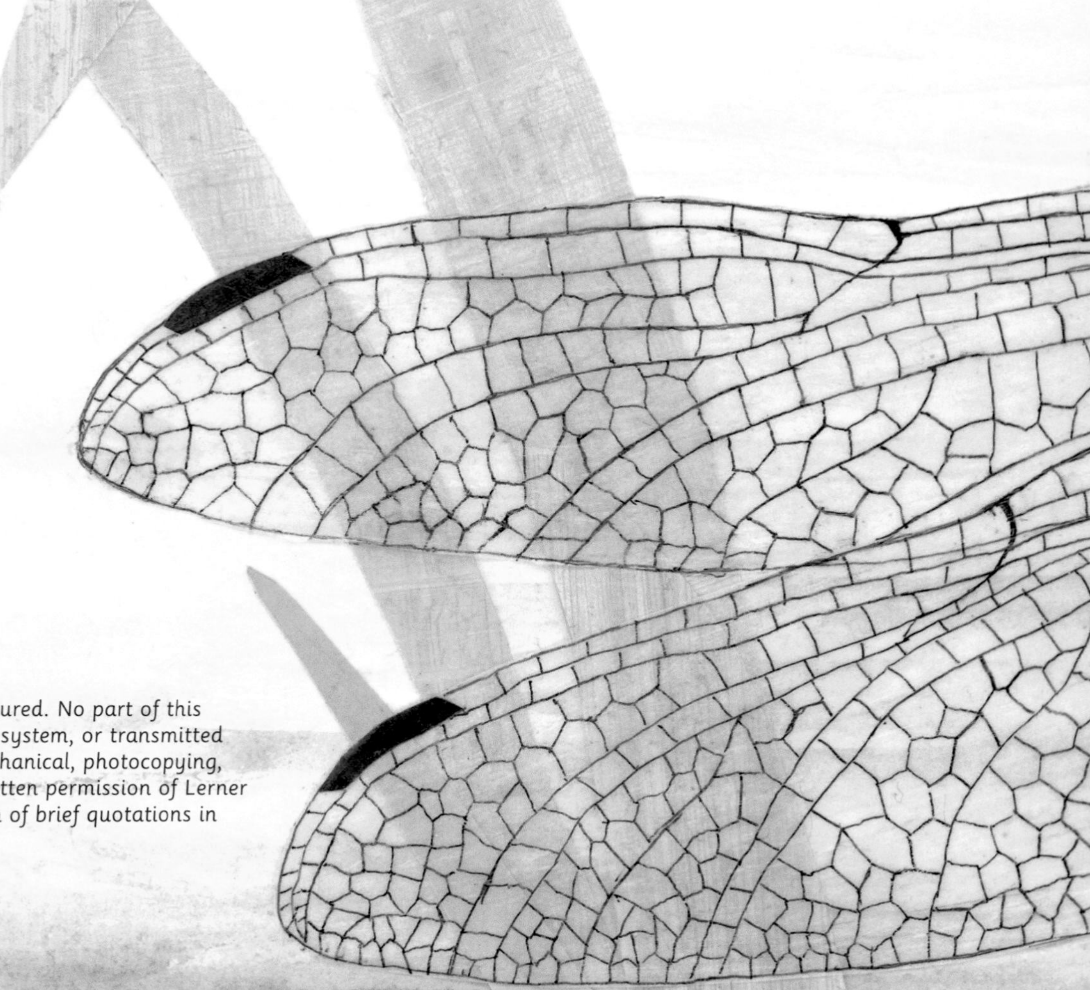

Millbrook Press
A division of Lerner Publishing Group, Inc.
241 First Avenue North
Minneapolis, MN 55401 U.S.A.

Website address: www.lernerbooks.com

Library of Congress Cataloging-in-Publication Data
Glaser, Linda.
Dazzling dragonflies : a life cycle story / by Linda Glaser ; illustrated by Mia Posada.
p. cm. — (Linda Glaser's classic creatures)
ISBN: 978-0-8225-6753-0 (lib. bdg. : alk. paper)
1. Dragonflies—Life cycles—Juvenile literature. I. Posada, Mia, ill. II. Title.
QL520.G53 2008
595.7'33—dc22 2007021886

Manufactured in the United States of America
1 2 3 4 5 6 – JR – 13 12 11 10 09 08

Hello, mama dragonfly!

You dip down to the water
and lay a clutch of eggs.

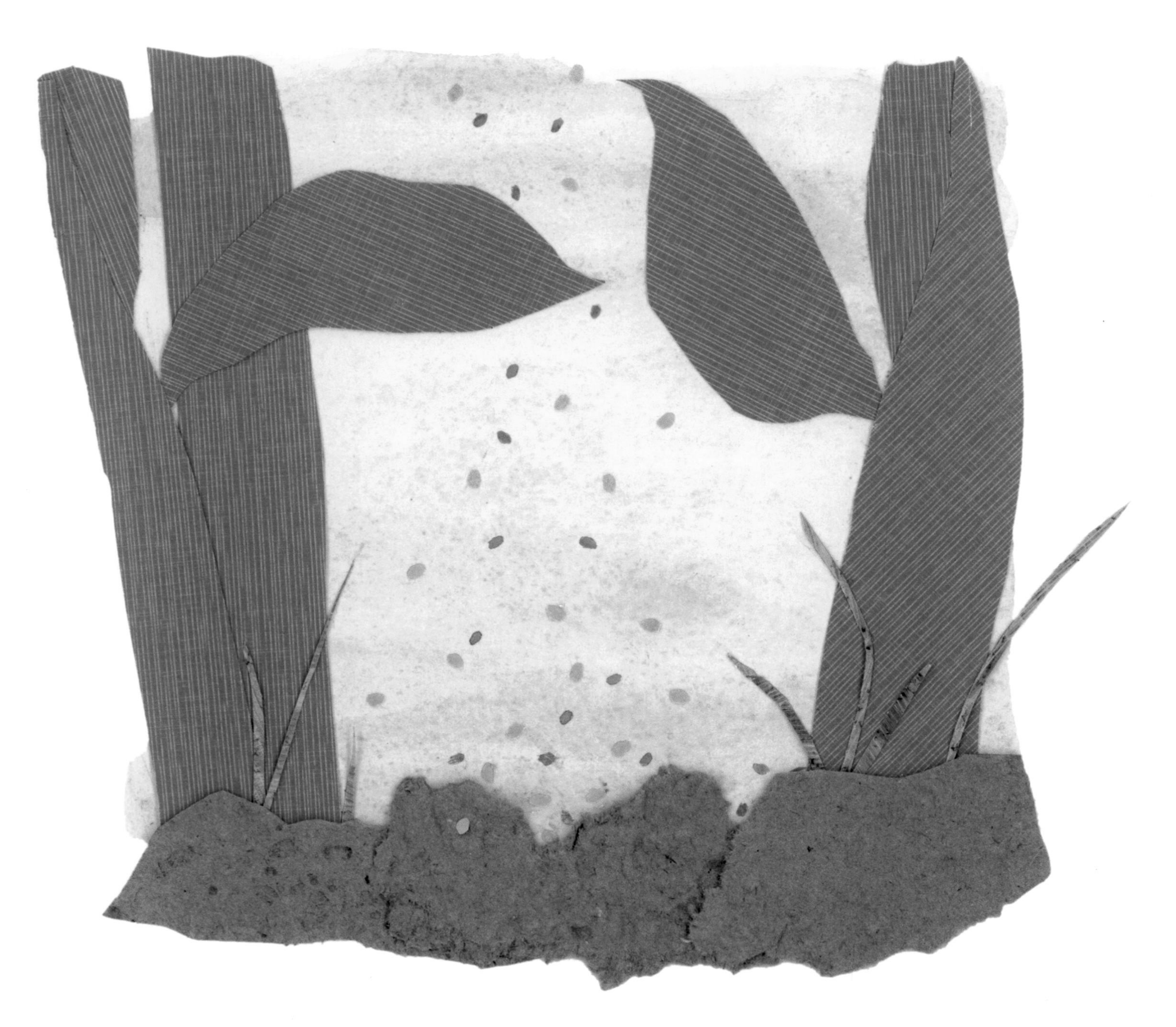

They sink to the bottom, safely hidden.

Soon they hatch into little nymphs.

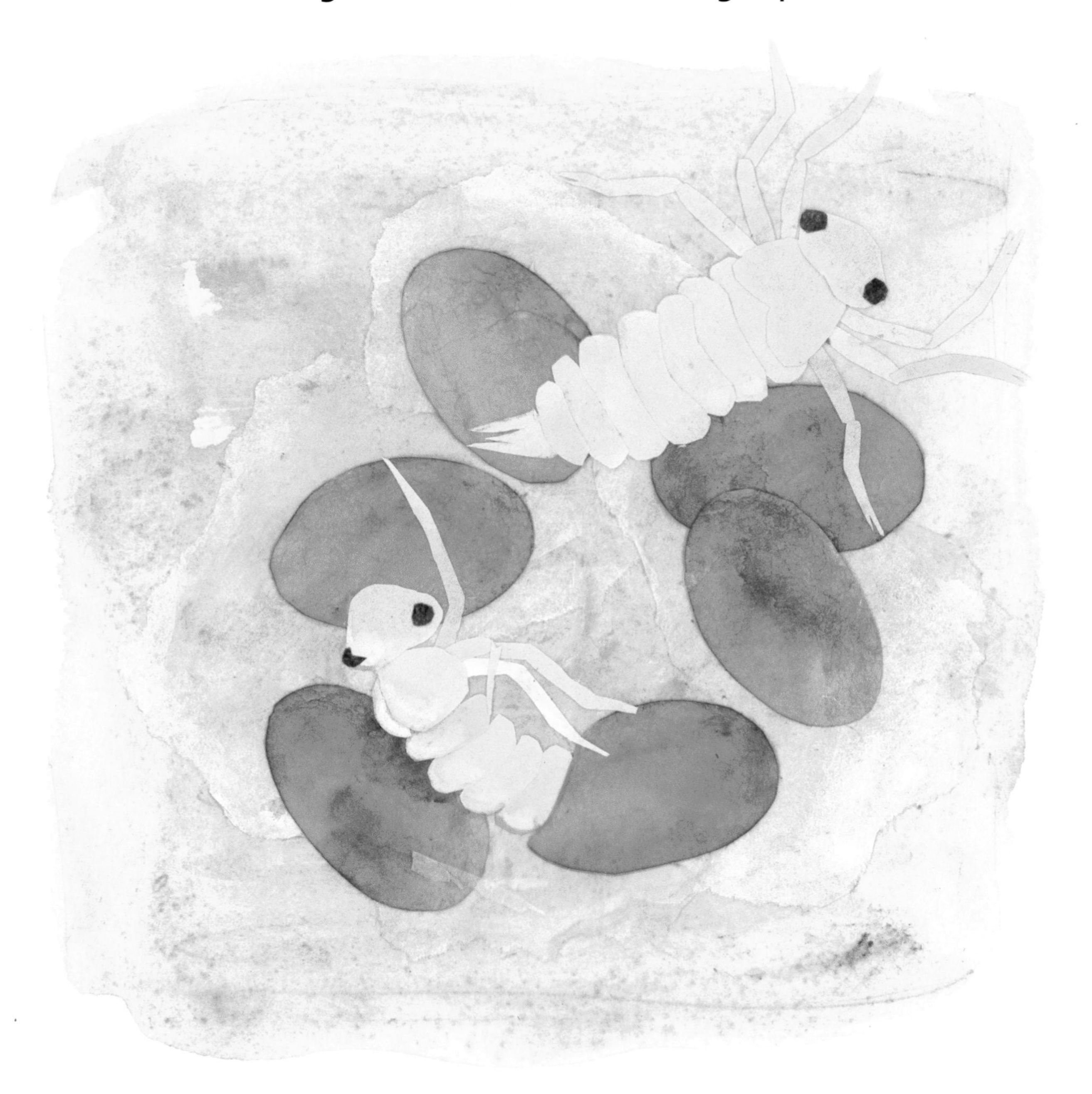

Hello, swimming dragonfly nymph!

Watch out—
here comes a hungry fish.

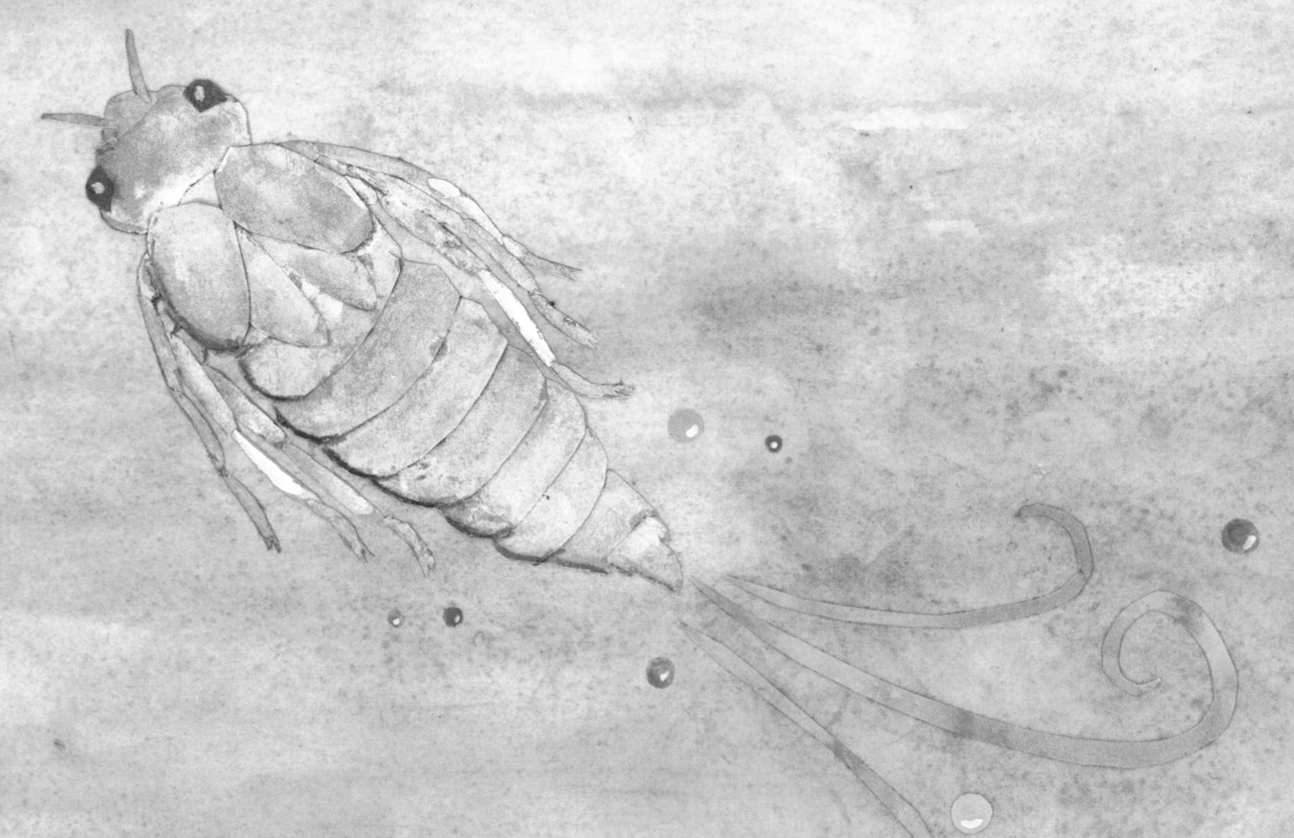

Whoosh! Water squirts through your gills,
and you whisk away—quick!
You look like a small swimming bug.
Where are your *wings*, little dragonfly nymph?

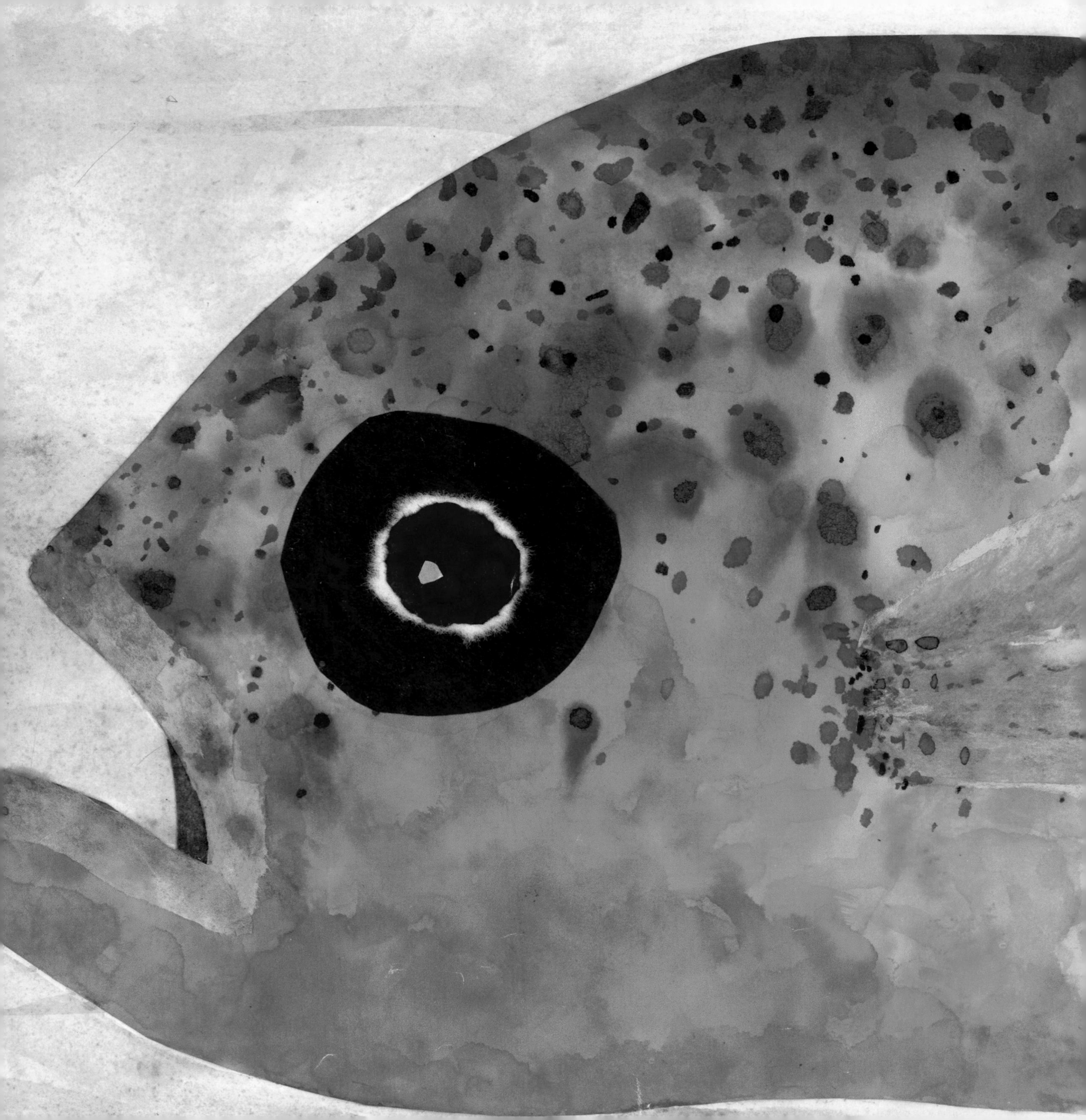

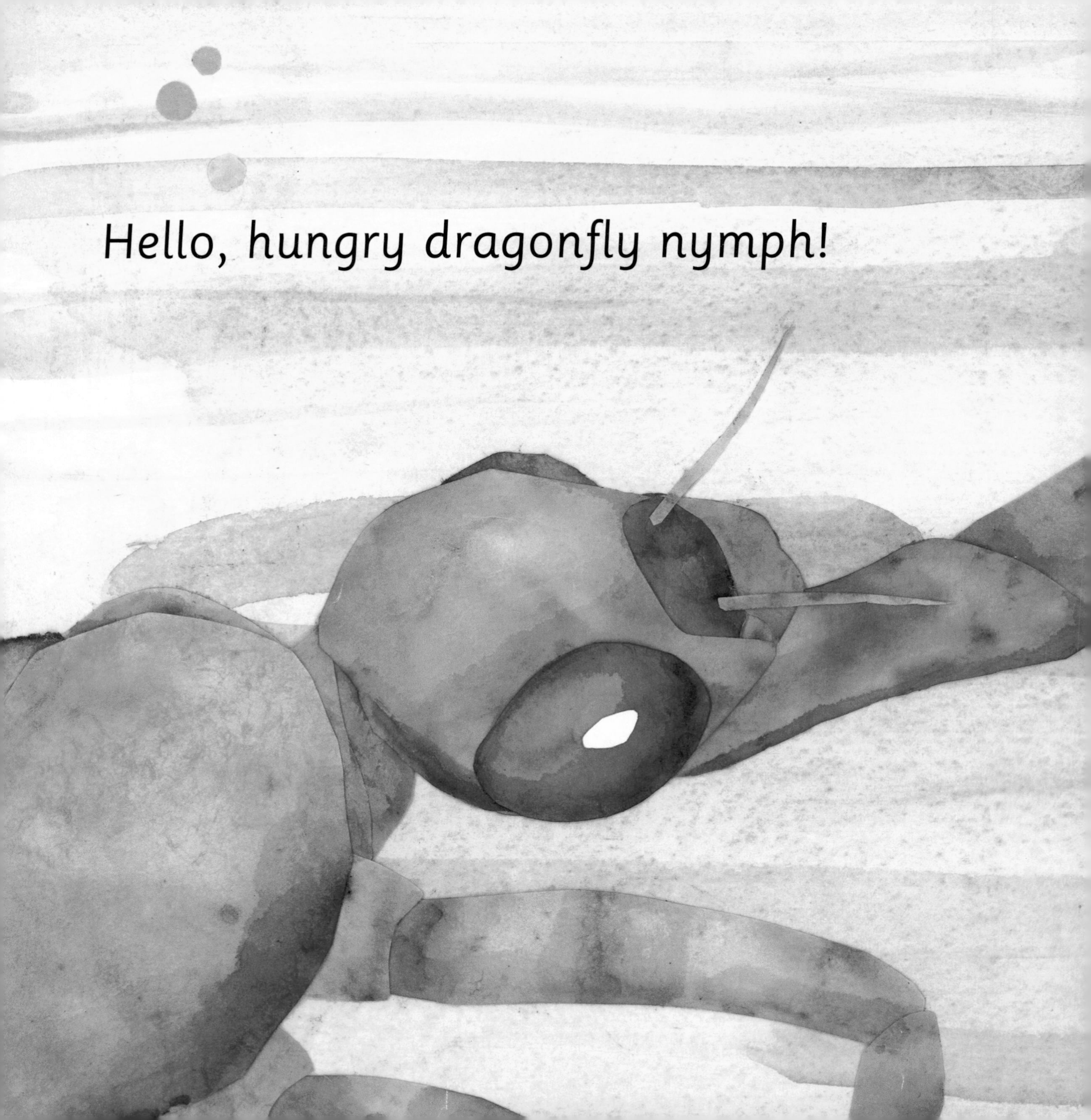

Hello, hungry dragonfly nymph!

You jut out your
long toothy lip
and grab small
bugs and fish.

You eat and eat and
grow and grow until...

you shed your little
nymph skin for a new
and bigger one.

But where are
your *wings*,
dragonfly nymph?

Hello, growing dragonfly nymph!

You shed your skin
again and again.
But still no wings.
Not quite. Not yet.
Until...

. . . early one morning,

you climb out of the
water and onto a stick.

One last time,
you shed your skin.
And look—
you have *wings*!

Are you ready to fly?
Not quite. Not yet.
You must stay very still
till your soft wings set.

You wait and wait.
Not quite. Not yet.

Then, at last, your four
flat wings are set.
Are you ready to fly?
Yes.
Finally, yes!

Hello, flying dragonfly!

Amazing acrobatic insect—
flitting and floating here
and there.
You dip and dive and dart,
then *zip*!

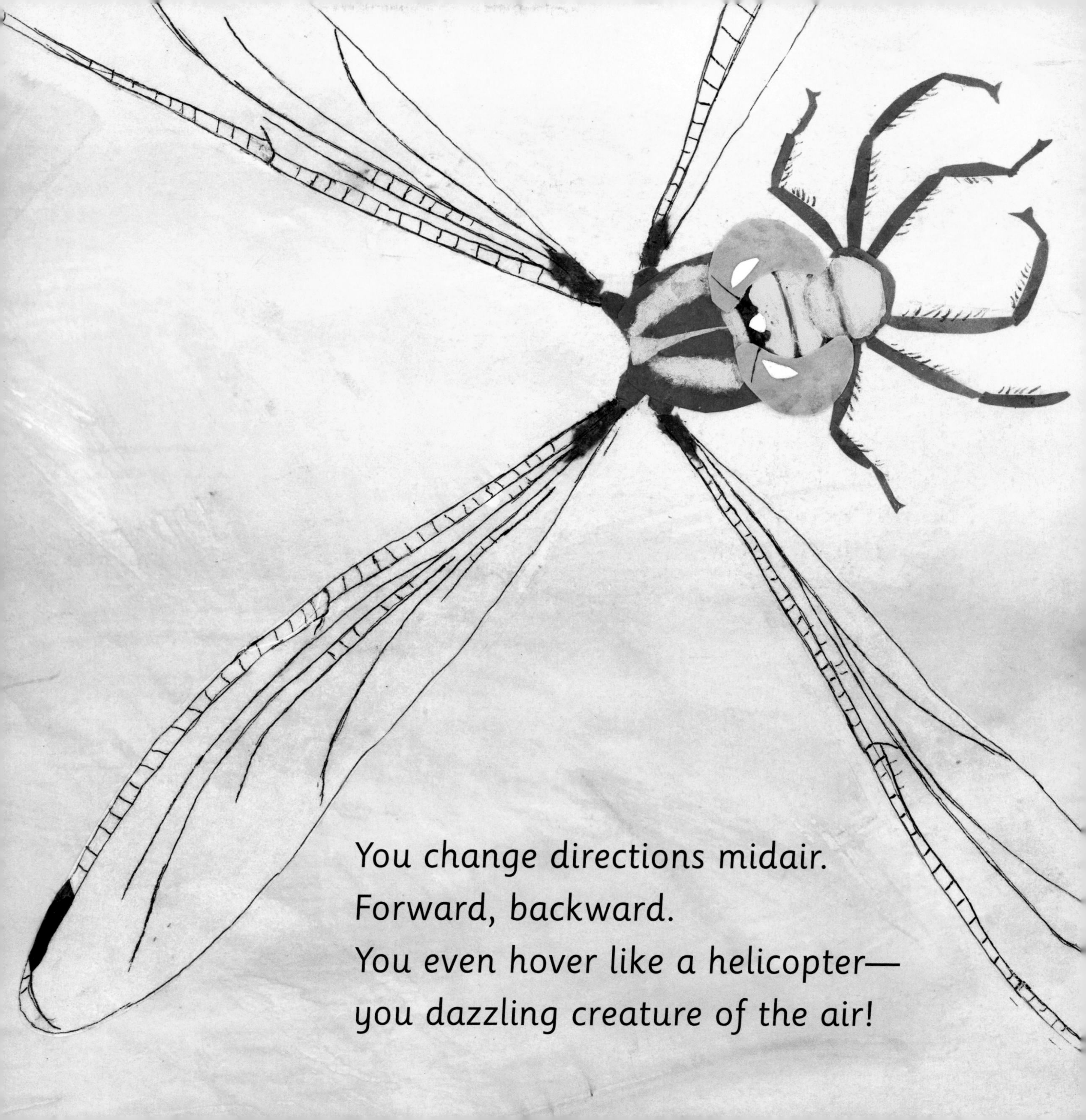

You change directions midair.
Forward, backward.
You even hover like a helicopter—
you dazzling creature of the air!

Hello, hungry dragonfly!

Your big, big eyes see all around.
You search for anything small that moves.
Mosquitoes, flies, beetles, bugs—
all are your food.

Look—a mosquito! From far away, you see it move.
Your keen eyes tell you it's flying food.
You fold your front legs like a tiny net.
In a flash, you are there. You catch it midair!

Hello, dancing dragonflies!

Way before dinosaurs, your ancestors thrived—
and to this day, dragonflies have survived!
Now you wheel and dance in the air together—
dragonfly partners sparking new life.

Hello, mama dragonfly!

Sun glitters on fresh welcoming water.
You dip down and lay your clutch of eggs.
Soon they'll hatch
and in time...

become new dragonflies!

Here are the answers to some questions you may have about dragonflies.

What dragonflies are pictured in the illustrations?

The illustrations show three types. All are common around the United States. They are:

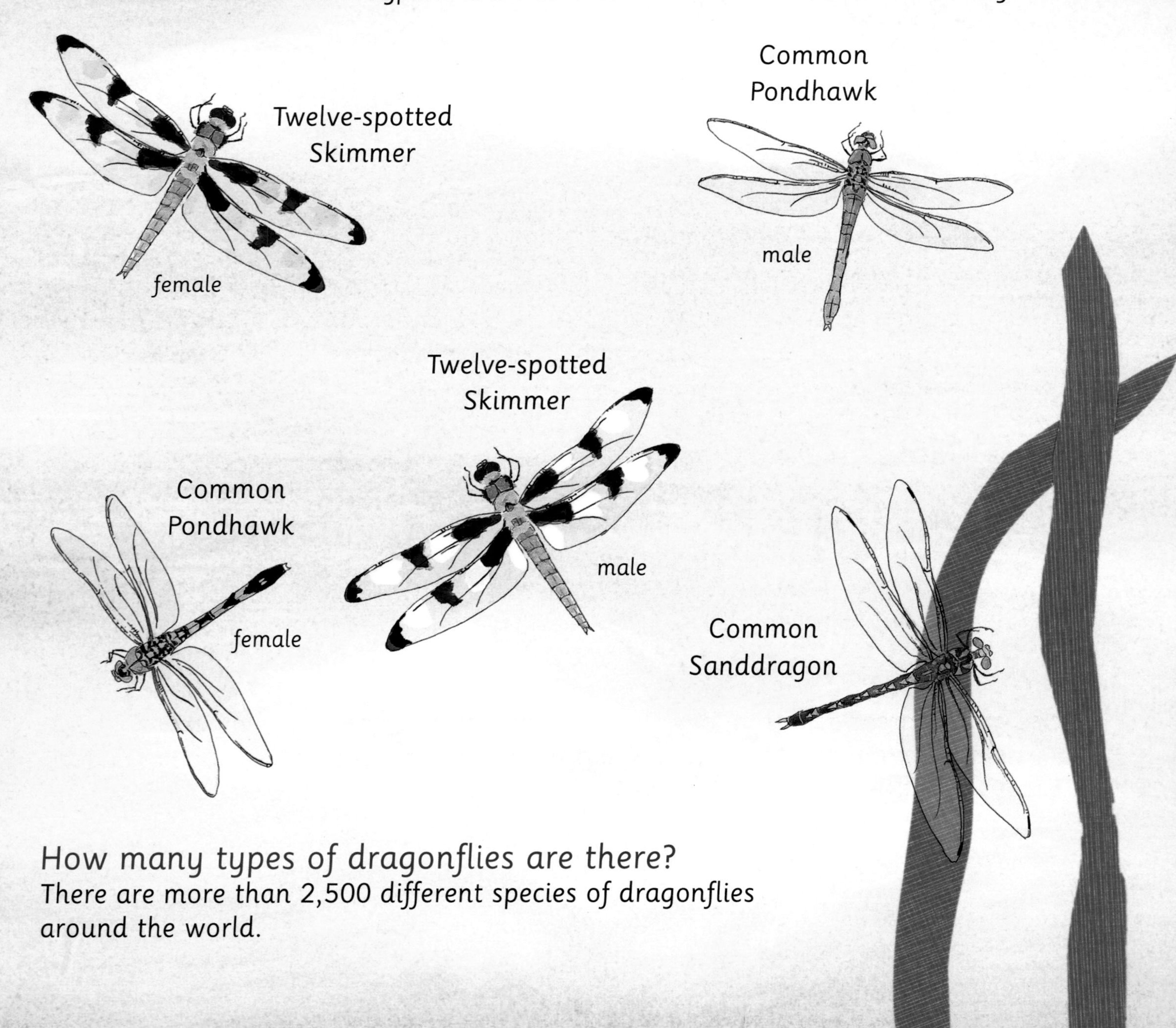

How many types of dragonflies are there?

There are more than 2,500 different species of dragonflies around the world.

How long have dragonflies lived on Earth?

Fossils show that dragonflies have lived on Earth for about 300 million years. That means they were here about 100 million years before dinosaurs! Dragonflies have survived longer than any other flying insects.

How have dragonflies survived for so long?

Some scientists believe that dragonflies have survived until the present because they don't depend on one certain body of water. They fly to new places to lay their eggs. This behavior causes them to spread out over a large area, which has helped them continue to survive. And they are excellent flying hunters. No other creature is better at hunting in the air. This is also important for survival.

Were ancient dragonflies the same as dragonflies today?

Prehistoric dragonflies were much bigger than dragonflies are today. Some had a wingspan (measured from wing tip to wing tip)of more than 3 feet (91 cm). They were the largest insects of any time. Modern dragonflies are still large insects. But they are much smaller than the prehistoric dragonflies. Their wingspan today is usually between 1 and 8 inches (2.5 and 20 cm).

What is a dragonfly nymph?

A dragonfly nymph is a baby dragonfly—also called a larva, or naiad. Dragonflies spend most of their lives as these water creatures. They spend a much shorter time as adult dragonflies with wings.

How long do dragonflies live?

This varies a great deal from one species of dragonfly to another. In general, the larva stage is from one to two years and the mature dragonfly stage (with wings) is about one and a half months.

Do the nymphs turn into adult dragonflies alone or in groups?

Usually, it's in groups. It's an amazing sight when perhaps hundreds or even thousands of dragonflies all emerge with their new glistening wings.

How do dragonflies see?

An adult dragonfly eye has about 30,000 lenses. This helps it to see in all directions and to notice the movement of a bug from far away.

How fast can dragonflies fly?

Some dragonflies can fly 30 miles (48 km) per hour. Their front and back wings work independently, which helps them switch directions very quickly.

Do dragonflies hurt people?

No. Dragonflies don't have stingers. They are quite harmless to people. They actually help people by eating pesky insects, such as flies and mosquitoes. However, if you catch a dragonfly, it may bite in self-defense—just as any captured animal might.

What animals eat dragonflies?

Dragonflies are an important part of the food chain. Fish, birds, and insects eat dragonfly nymphs. Birds eat adult dragonflies. And large dragonflies eat smaller ones.

Where are dragonflies found?

Dragonflies are found all over the world in ponds, lakes, rivers, streams, marshes, and other wetlands. Although most dragonflies are not endangered, some of their habitats are becoming polluted. And many wetlands have been drained for development. Like all animals, dragonflies need plenty of clean, safe habitats in order to survive. Where dragonflies are plentiful, it indicates that the nearby water is clean. Hopefully, dragonflies will continue to brighten our planet for another 300 million years.

For more information about dragonflies, visit this dragonfly website:
http://powell.colgate.edu/wda/Beginners_Guide.htm.